theory for
piano students

by LORA BENNER

BOOK
TWO

ED. 2522

G. SCHIRMER, Inc.

DISTRIBUTED BY

HAL•LEONARD®
CORPORATION
7777 W. BLUEMOUND RD. P.O. BOX 13819 MILWAUKEE, WI 53213

FOREWORD

This book provides theoretic knowledge, writing, and playing experience in musical subjects which are related to the second year of piano study. It is also of use in the study of theory for the second year without regard to instrument.

Scales, scale degrees, key signatures, key tones, intervals, triads, seventh chords, and cadences are in major keys.

The scope of the material may be increased by additional writing, playing, and singing.

The importance of meter and phrasing and the knowledge of song form may be shown with further examples.

The material is presented in lessons and work sheets to be completed in an eight or nine month term of private or class instruction.

L. B.

CONTENTS

Examples of intervals, chords and cadences are in a very few keys. These may be written in other keys on separate music paper and played on the piano.

Lesson One
SCALES
WHOLE TONE, CHROMATIC, DIATONIC

A **SCALE** is a LADDER. Scales are tones of music arranged in one direction.

Knowing scales is important for many reasons. The main two are:

1 Knowing scales makes all other music study easier.
2 Most music is written on tones of some scale.

There are many kinds of scales:

The **WHOLE TONE SCALE** has all WHOLE STEPS

      C   D   E   F♯   G♯   A♯   C

The **CHROMATIC SCALE** has all HALF STEPS

UP C C♯ D D♯ E F F♯ G G♯ A A♯ B C

Write these chromatic notes from Middle C up. Play this scale on the piano with one finger to see how it sounds.

DOWN C B B♭ A A♭ G G♭ F E E♭ D D♭ C

Write these chromatic notes from Middle C down. Play them with one finger.

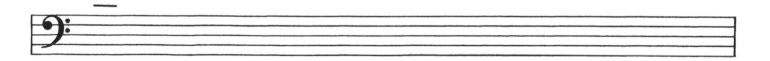

KEY TONE or **TONIC** are the names for *do* or 1.

The **DIATONIC SCALE** has both WHOLE STEPS and HALF STEPS.

DIA means through, **TONIC** means tone. There is ONE and only one of each **tone** (or letter name) in the diatonic scale.

There are 8 notes in a scale of one octave. Each note is a **SCALE DEGREE.**

    1 2 3 4 5 6 7 8. A Degree is a number.

In the MAJOR Diatonic Scale, HALF-STEPS are between 3 and 4; 7 and 8.
    The others are WHOLE STEPS.

THIS IS THE PATTERN....... Half-steps 3-4 and 7-8

Play the diatonic scale on the piano starting with C. There are WHITE key half-steps
    between E-F (3-4) and B-C (7-8)

    Start on G. You must play F♯ for the 7-8 half-step.

    Start on D. You must keep the F♯ and add C♯ for the pattern.

    Start on A. You must keep F♯ and C♯ and add G♯.

In Sharp Scales, the NEW SHARP is always 7 *(ti)*.

    Write the scale of D on the staff below. Use accidentals.

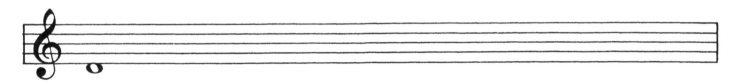

In Flat Scales, the **NEW** flat is always 4 *(fa)* for the 3-4 half-step.

    Write the scale of F on the staff below.

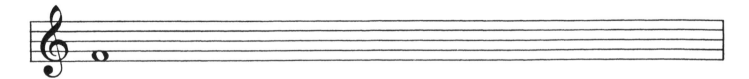

    Write the scale of B♭. Use accidentals.

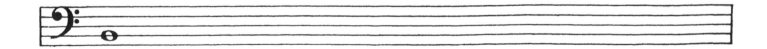

Tap out the rhythm of the notes below. Do you recognize it? If you do not know what it is at first try tapping again. It is a familiar song of the West.

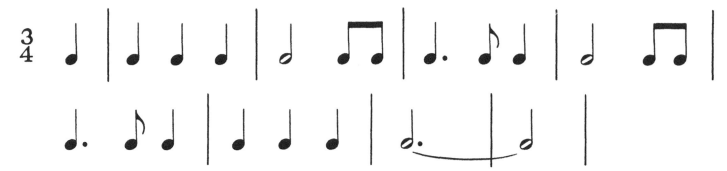

On the staff below put in the time signature. Notice the slurs and phrases.

On the staff below, put in the time signature and the phrasing slurs.

Play both of these lines of melody. Notice that they both have incomplete measures at the beginning and at the end. These incomplete measures add up to one measure for each melody.

In what key is the lower melody written?

4

Work Sheet

1 What is a SCALE? _____

2 Name three kinds of scales.

    a _____

    b _____

    c _____

3 Why is it important to know scales?

_____

4 What kind of scale is written below?

5 On the staff below, write this scale going down.

6 What does the word DIATONIC mean? _____

7 What kinds of steps are found in Diatonic scales?

_____

8 In the Scale of G which DEGREE is sharped? _____

9 In the Scale of F which DEGREE is flatted? _____

10 Write the scale of F on the staff below. Use whole notes.

Lesson Two

MAJOR SCALES

CIRCLE OF FIFTHS   TETRACHORDS

There are 15 key signatures for music written in major keys.

C — no sharps or flats

G — 1 sharp	F — 1 flat
D — 2 sharps	B♭ — 2 flats
A — 3 sharps	E♭ — 3 flats
E — 4 sharps	A♭ — 4 flats
B — 5 sharps	D♭ — 5 flats
F♯ — 6 sharps	G♭ — 6 flats
C♯ — 7 sharps	C♭ — 7 flats

Since there are only **12 tones** on which to build scales, some of these scales must be ENHARMONIC.   En = same, Harmonic = tonality.

ENHARMONIC — same tone different note name.

B and C♭, F♯ and G♭, C♯ and D♭ are enharmonic.

There are many ways to show the relationship of the keys. One way is the

CIRCLE OF FIFTHS
(or DOMINANT CIRCLE)

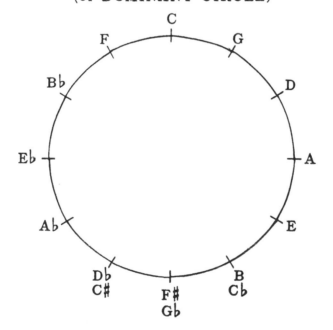

In Lesson one the **SCALE PATTERN** was based on the OCTAVE approach:

Half-steps between 3-4 and 7-8. The others are whole steps.

The TETRACHORD is another way. A TETRACHORD is 4 tones of a major scale, half an octave.

The **TETRACHORD PATTERN** is a whole step, whole step, half-step. There are TWO tetrachords in a major scale. They are joined by a whole step.

First tetrachord (half) 1, 2, 3, 4 or do, re, mi, fa.

Second tetrachord (half) 5, 6, 7, 8 or sol, la, ti, do.

The following chart shows how Major Scales in SHARPS are related:

C̲ D E F - G A B C
       G̲ A B C - D E F♯ G
           D̲ E F♯ G - A B C♯ D
               A̲ B C♯ D - E F♯ G♯ A
                    E̲ F♯ G♯ A - B C♯ D♯ E
                         B̲ C♯ D♯ E - F♯ G♯ A♯ B
                               F̲♯ G♯ A♯ B - C♯ D♯ E♯ F♯
                                   C♯ D♯ E♯ F♯

The second tetrachord of any scale in sharps is the same as the first tetrachord of the scale having *one more sharp*.

The following chart shows how Major Scales in FLATS are related:

C̲♭ D♭ E♭ F♭ - G♭ A♭ B♭ C♭
       G̲♭ A♭ B♭ C♭ - D♭ E♭ F G♭
           D̲♭ E♭ F G♭ - A♭ B♭ C D♭
               A̲♭ B♭ C D♭ - E♭ F G A♭
                    E̲♭ F G A♭ - B♭ C D E♭
                         B̲♭ C D E♭ - F G A B♭
                              F̲ G A B♭ - C D E F
                                     C̲ D E F

The second tetrachord of any scale in flats is the same as the first tetrachord of the scale having *one less flat*.

Notice how the Keytones match the Circle of Fifths.

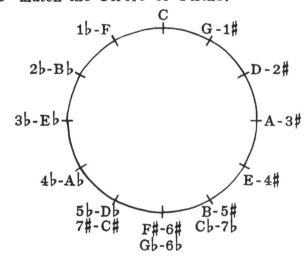

On the staff below, draw a line under each tetrachord. There are two sets which are the same. Mark the first set *a* and the second set *b*.

On the staff below, draw a line under each tetrachord. Mark the two sets *a* and *b*.

Knowing key relationships makes learning music much easier. Many pieces have sections which are in a different key from the key signature. You can tell by the accidentals.

If you are learning a piece in the Key of C and find an F♯, that section of the piece is in the key of G. If you are learning a piece in the key of F and find a B♮, that section of the piece is in the key of C.

Here are four measures from the *Soldier's March* by Robert Schumann. Play this music and notice the accidental C♯ for the section which is in the key of D although the key signature is the key of G.

Did you recognize *Home On The Range* from the rhythm tapping in Lesson 1? In the melody below, some of the notes are missing. Draw notes in where they belong. Be sure to get the right pitch for the notes and the right KIND of note for the correct number of beats.

In what KEY was the above written?

Draw in the missing notes for this melody in the Key of F.

Play both of these on the piano.

Work Sheet

1   What is the PATTERN of a Major Scale?

   _____

2   What is the PATTERN of a Tetrachord?

   _____

3   How many tetrachords are there in an octave scale? _____

4   What kind of step joins them? _____

5   What scale degree (number) becomes the key tone of the next scale in the circle of

   fifths? _____

6   Give the name and number of sharps or flats for the 3 sets of enharmonic scales

   _____ _____ sharps and _____ _____ flats

   _____ _____ sharps and _____ _____ flats

   _____ _____ sharps and _____ _____ flats

7   What is the greatest number of sharps or flats in a key signature? _____

8   Name the following scale on the staff with the treble clef. _____

   Name the following scale on the staff with the bass clef. _____

   Draw lines under the tetrachords which have the same notes.

Work Sheet

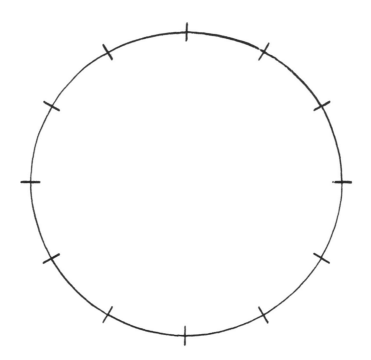

9   Write the **KEY TONES** in the circle above.

10 By what two names is the circle known?

_____

11 Write in the number of sharps or flats for the 15 major key signatures given

C _____   G _____   D _____   A _____   E _____   B _____

F♯ _____   C♯ _____   F _____   B♭ _____   E♭ _____   A♭ _____

D♭ _____   G♭ _____   C♭ _____

12 How many scale degrees are there? _____

13 What is the other name for KEY TONE? _____

14 How many of each letter name are in a diatonic scale? _____

Lesson Three

KEY SIGNATURES AND SCALES

Key Signatures are the Sharps and Flats at the beginning of each staff. They are placed in the order they appear.

They are placed only on lines and spaces of the staff or the space above or below the staff.

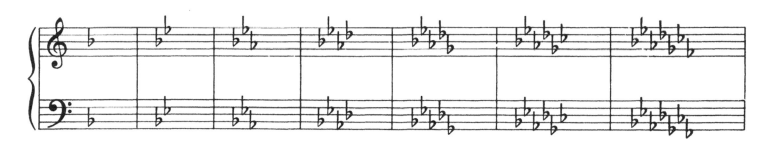

✗ is a double sharp sign. It raises the note a WHOLE STEP.

♭♭ is a double flat sign. It lowers the note a WHOLE STEP.

Play $\begin{bmatrix} C\,\text{✗}, \\ A♭♭ \\ F\,\text{✗} \\ E♭♭ \end{bmatrix}$ you will find it enharmonic to $\begin{bmatrix} D. \\ G. \\ G. \\ D. \end{bmatrix}$

Write enharmonic notes for the following:

C✗ _____ C♯ _____ E♭♭ _____ E♭ _____ F✗ _____ G✗ _____ G♭♭ _____ A✗ _____

A♭♭ _____ B♭ _____ B♯ _____ D♭♭ _____ D _____ F _____ C _____ D✗ _____

12

On the staffs below: Write the Major Scales which have sharps.
Do NOT put in a key signature but use ac-
cidentals before the notes for the major
scale pattern.
Write one octave up and down
G Major is given.

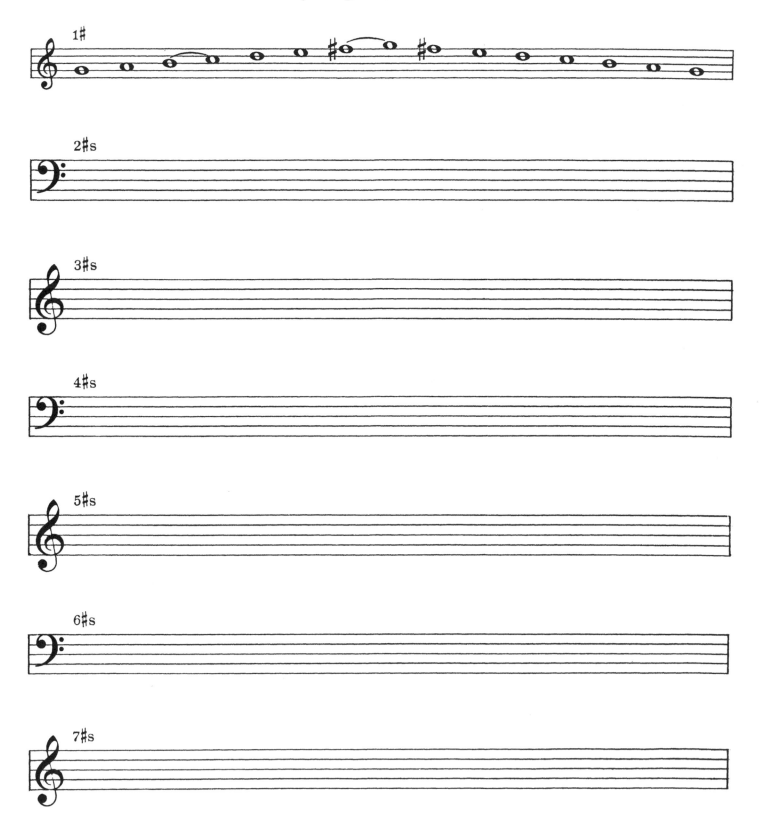

On the staffs below: Write the Major Scales which have flats.
Do NOT put in a key signature but use
accidentals before the notes for the major
scale pattern.
Write one octave up and down.

14

On the staffs below: Write the Key Signatures for
all the Major Scales except C.
Write each Key Tone.

NAMES OF SCALE DEGREES

Each scale degree has a special name:

1. Tonic I
2. Supertonic II
3. Mediant III
4. Subdominant IV
5. Dominant V
6. Submediant VI
7. Subtonic or Leading Tone VII

Of these the **TONIC** – (I), **DOMINANT** – (V), and **SUBDOMINANT** – (IV) are the most important. Notice that Roman numerals are used for the scale degrees.

In the Scale of C which note is the Dominant? _____

Subdominant? _____

In the Scale of G name the Tonic _____

Dominant _____

Subdominant _____

On the staff below write the scale one octave for the Key signature given. Write I, V, and IV under the proper notes.

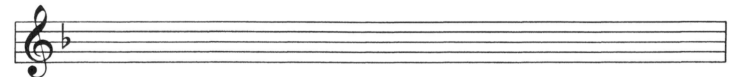

Write the key signature and put I, IV, and V under the proper notes.

Write the I, IV, and V notes after each signature below. Use whole notes.

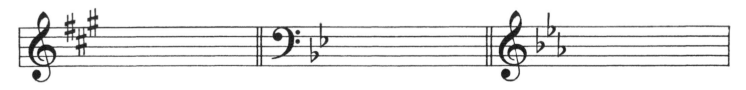

Here is a rhythm to tap. Can you name this song? It is a well-known Christmas carol.

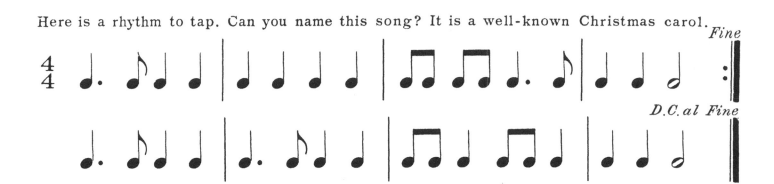

On the staffs below, two measures of the song are given with the syllable names. Can you finish writing in the notes with the time value of the tapping exercise? Play and sing the notes with the syllable names.

Did you write the melody in the correct key? Now write the same melody in the Key of G. Play and sing it.

Work Sheet

1   What is a Key Signature?

2   On the staff below, write key signatures in sharps for the key tones (tonics) given.

3   Write in the key tones for the signatures given below.

4   Write the scale of A on the staff below and mark I, IV, and V under the correct notes.

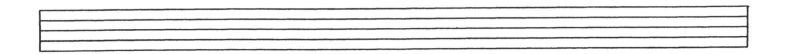

5   On the staff below, write in the key signatures in flats for the key tones given.

45471

Lesson Four
BEAT   PHRASING   SONG FORM

A **BEAT** is the TIME UNIT of a composition.

Some beats are strong, some are weak. An orchestra conductor puts his baton or hand
down for a strong beat and up for a weak beat.

$\frac{4}{4}$ time = 4 beats in a measure.

A quarter note gets one beat. (is the beat unit)

Beat 1 is strong, beat 3 almost as strong.

Beats 2 and 4 are weak.

$\frac{3}{4}$ time = 3 beats in a measure. A quarter note is the beat unit.

Beat 1 is strong.

Beats 2 and 3 are weak.

$\frac{2}{4}$ time = 2 beats in a measure. A quarter note is the beat unit.

Beat 1 is strong.

Beat 2 is weak.

METER is another way of saying TIME. METER is the way note values and accents
are grouped in a measure.

SIMPLE TIME or **SIMPLE METER** has 2, 3, or 4 as the top figure of the
time signature.

Music may be begun on any beat in a measure. Since meter is the way notes and accents
are grouped in a measure, the same notes will have different rhythms depending
on which beat begins the music. There are as many meters as beats in a measure.
In $\frac{4}{4}$ time there are 4 different meters.

Play the example below. Count as you play and accent the first beat of each measure.
Notice the difference of each to the others.

ALLA BREVE is the time signature of $\frac{2}{2}$, 2 beats in a measure with a half-note as the beat unit, and is shown by the sign ¢. It indicates quick time and has been called cut time because the **C** has been cut to ¢ and the $\frac{4}{4}$ to $\frac{2}{2}$.

MELODIC LINE - the way the melody moves.

PHRASE - Part of the melodic line.
    There is a natural break or pause at the end of a phrase.

When we speak or sing, we pause at certain places. The following example of *My Bonnie* will show this.

    My Bonnie lies over the ocean, (slight pause)
    My Bonnie lies over the sea, (slight pause)
    My Bonnie lies over the ocean, (slight pause)
    Oh bring back my Bonnie to me. (definite end)

We do not pause at other places. We do not say **My Bonnie lies over,** (pause) the ocean my, (pause) Bonnie lies, (pause) etc.

Music without words also has these slight pauses at the end of each phrase. Playing this way – with a good understanding of the phrases in music – is called **PHRASING**.

PHRASING – the clear playing of PHRASES.

Usually there are slurs over or under phrases. A phrase often starts on an *up* beat.

Here is part of *My Bonnie* to play with the idea of phrases.

We know from Book 1 that music has three main features:

MELODY HARMONY RHYTHM

Melody is made up of ideas or **THEMES**.

SONG FORM is the PATTERN of the THEMES.

In Lesson 3 we wrote *Deck The Halls*. This song has two themes which are easy to find.

The first 4 measures are one theme. It is called theme A.
The second 4 measures are the same. It is also theme A.
The third 4 measures are different. They are called theme B.
The last 4 measures are like the first. They are theme A.

So the SONG FORM of *Deck The Halls* is A A B A.

Old MacDonald has the same Song Form as have many other compositions including
Sonatas and Symphonies.

If you can find the themes in the music you play, you will learn it more easily and
play it much better.

Here is *Oh Susanna*. Measure Accents are given. These are the FIRST beat of each measure. Draw in the bar-lines before the accented notes. Finish putting stems on the notes. Watch their time values! Write in the key and time signatures. Play it on the piano.

Next is *Old Folks at Home* (Swanee River). Here there is a slight change in the first two themes, but they are both still called A and the PATTERN is A A B A. Add notes to complete the melody and play this song.

Work Sheet

1   What is a BEAT? _____

2   Is a DOWN beat weak or strong? _____

3   What is another name for TIME? _____

4   What are the TOP figures in SIMPLE TIME signature?

_____   _____   _____

5   What beats can begin a piece in $\frac{4}{4}$ time?

_____   _____   _____   _____

6   Which is the strongest beat? _____

7   What is a PHRASE? _____

8   What do you do at the end of a phrase? _____

_____

9   What is PHRASING? _____

_____

10 How is the time signature of Alla Breve shown? _____

11 What beats can begin a piece in $\frac{2}{4}$ time? _____

12 In the following put in bar lines to show DIFFERENT meter forms.

13 What is SONG FORM? _____

_____

14 What alphabet letter is used for the first theme? _____

15 What alphabet letter is used for the second theme? _____

Lesson Five

TRIADS   POSITIONS OF TRIADS

In Book I we learned the alphabet by THIRDS – the CHORD ALPHABET

A C E G B D F A C E G B D F A etc.

Any three notes of the alphabet by thirds in succession form a three note chord
a **TRIAD**

In the spaces below, write in the missing letters to form triads. Left to Right.

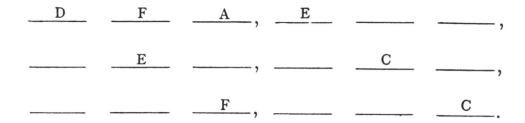

Triads may be played two ways:

    Harmonically – all at once (solid)

    Melodically – one note at a time (broken)

Broken triads are written with one note following another.

Rolled triads are written with a wavy line before the solid chord.

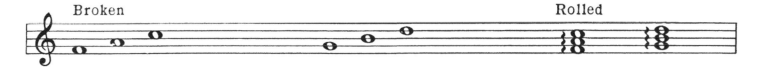

On the staffs below, fill in the missing upper notes to form solid triads.

Every chord has as many **POSITIONS** as it has tones.

A TRIAD has three tones; therefore it has three positions.

Here is the chord C E G in three positions. Play them on the piano.

When ⌈ C ⌉ is the lowest note, the chord is in ⌈ **ROOT POSITION** ⌉
      | E | | **FIRST INVERSION** |
      ⌊ G ⌋   ⌊ **SECOND INVERSION** ⌋

In Book 1 we learned that an INTERVAL is the difference between two notes and that
the top and bottom notes are counted in order to MEASURE the INTERVAL.

When a TRIAD is in **ROOT POSITION**, the three letters of the chord alphabet
are in order, every other letter.

The interval from the bottom note to the middle note is a third.
The interval from the bottom note to the top note is a fifth.

Write two notes above each note given below to form a triad in ROOT position. Then
play the chords on the piano and listen to their sound.

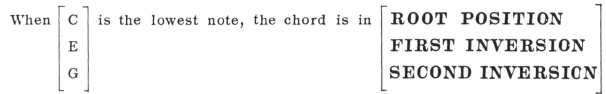

A   B   C   D   E   F   G   A

When a TRIAD is in the **FIRST INVERSION**, the three letters of the chord
alphabet are not every other letter, not in order.

The interval from the bottom note to the middle note is a third.
The interval from the bottom note to the top note is a sixth.
This is called a 6 chord. (Since thirds and fifths are normal chord intervals,
they are not mentioned.)

Write two notes above each of the following notes to form 6 chords. Then play the
chords and listen to their sound.

A6   B6   C6   D6   E6   F6   G6   A6

When a TRIAD is in the **SECOND INVERSION**, the three letters of the chord
alphabet are not in order. (Only in root position are they in order.)

The interval from the bottom note to the middle note is a fourth.
The interval from the bottom note to the top note is a sixth.
This is called a $^6_4$ chord.

Write two notes above each of the following notes to form $^6_4$ chords.
Then play the chords and listen to their sound.

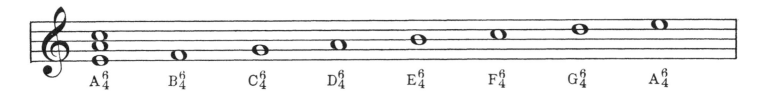

A^6_4 B^6_4 C^6_4 D^6_4 E^6_4 F^6_4 G^6_4 A^6_4

Write triads in three positions for each of the following:

Key of C

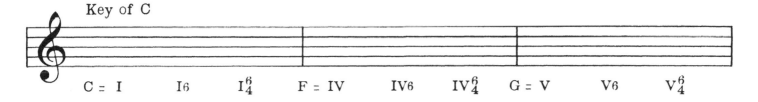

C = I   I6 I^6_4 F = IV   IV6 IV^6_4 G = V   V6 V^6_4

In the Key of C, the triad on C and its inversions is the **TONIC TRIAD**.
The triad on F and its inversions is the **SUBDOMINANT TRIAD**.
The triad on G and its inversions is the **DOMINANT TRIAD**.

In the Key of G, the I, IV and V chords are on G, C and D.
Write them on the following staff.

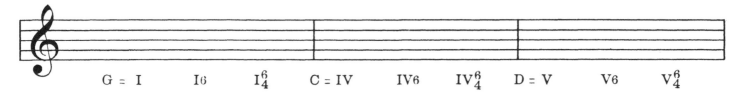

G = I   I6 I^6_4 C = IV   IV6 IV^6_4 D = V   V6 V^6_4

We can play many songs by using these three chords with the melody. And we can easily
play the same songs in other keys by playing the I, IV and V chords in other
keys with the melody played in the keys of the tonic chords.

This is called **TRANSPOSITION**. Transposition is writing, singing, or playing
music in different pitches (keys.)

Here is *Silent Night*. Notice that the V and IV chords are in positions which make the least movement. Play this. If you wish to transpose it, notice that the melody begins on *sol* and the harmony with the I chord in root position. Try it in the keys of G, F and others.

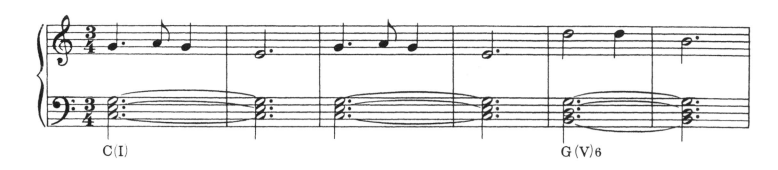

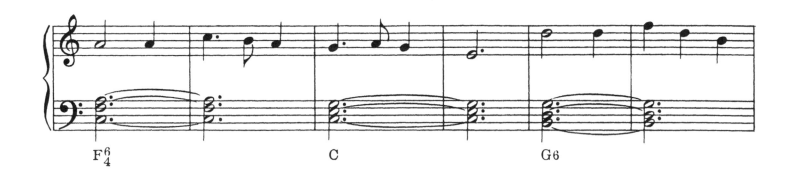

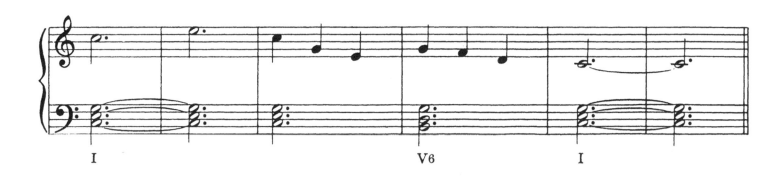

Work Sheet

1 What is a TRIAD?

2 Form triads on the letters given. ___F___ _____ _ _____

___ ___B___ _____ , _____ _____ ___B___

3 How many positions does a triad have? _____

4 What are the two intervals for ROOT POSITION?

_____ _____

5 What are the two intervals for FIRST INVERSION?

_____ _____

6 Which interval number is written to show this inversion?_____

7 What are the two intervals for SECOND INVERSION?

_____ _____

8 How are the two numbers written to show this inversion? _____

9 Give the Roman numerals for the three most important triads in any key.

_____ _____ _____

10 On the staff below, write the bass clef sign and the key signature for the Key of **F**. Then write the chords and their inversions.

$$\text{I} \quad \text{I6} \quad \text{I}^6_4 \quad \text{IV} \quad \text{IV6} \quad \text{IV}^6_4 \quad \text{V} \quad \text{V6} \quad \text{V}^6_4$$

11 On the following staff, write F A C as a broken chord and as a rolled chord.

12 On the staff below, write the treble clef sign and the key signature for the Key of **D**. Then write the chords and their inversions.

$$\text{I} \quad \text{I6} \quad \text{I}^6_4 \quad \text{IV} \quad \text{IV6} \quad \text{IV}^6_4 \quad \text{V} \quad \text{V6} \quad \text{V}^6_4$$

Lesson Six

PIANOS   PITCH   INTERVALS

Pianos have strings which are stretched over a **SOUNDING BOARD.**

A device called the **ACTION** has hammers at one end which hit the strings to produce the sound. The other end of the action is at the keys.

The **DAMPER PEDAL** lifts the dampers (felt pieces) from the strings which causes the strings to vibrate together.

The **SOFT PEDAL** on a GRAND piano shifts the action so the hammers hit only one string (una corda).

The **SOFT PEDAL** on other piano styles has the action move the hammers closer to the strings. They strike with less force and make the tone softer.

The **MIDDLE PEDAL** on a Grand piano is called the SOSTENUTO pedal because it sustains the notes played when it is pressed and holds them until it is released. It is used when the hands can not hold those keys and play others at the same time. It does not hold the other notes played.

Many modern pianos have no middle pedal. When there is a middle pedal on a spinet or vertical piano, it may be a practice pedal. This makes the tones very soft. Or it may be a type of sustaining pedal. On some older instruments, it made the tones have an odd sound like the old barroom pianos in Western Movies.

ABSOLUTE PITCH. The ability to recognize and to name a tone without knowing — except by the EAR — what the tone is. Some people are born with it. Others may get it from playing and hearing music. It is NOT necessary to have ABSOLUTE PITCH to be a good musician. Many great musicians did not have it.

RELATIVE PITCH. The ability to name a tone after hearing another tone. For example, if someone plays Middle C and tells you what it is, you should be able to recognize the E above it because of the relationship of the tones — the INTERVAL.

RELATIVE PITCH is absolutely necessary for all musicians.

On the staff below is a review of the intervals in the Key of C. Play them and listen
to their sounds.

Can you sing them on key without the piano?

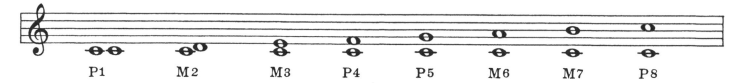

Intervals within any MAJOR key are either MAJOR or PERFECT.

The **PERFECT INTERVALS** are 1, 4, 5, 8. They are called Prime, Fourth, Fifth,
Octave and are written P1, P4, P5, P8.

On the staff below, write Perfect Intervals over the notes given. Be sure to count the upper and lower notes to write the size of the interval correctly.

On the following staff are Perfect Intervals. Write their size under them.

Here are more intervals to write. Each one is in a different key. Call the lower note *do*
of the Major Key for each interval and write a note above it to make the size given.

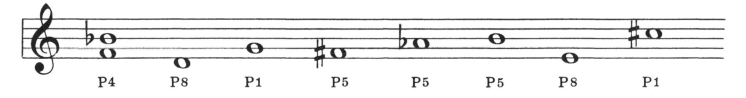

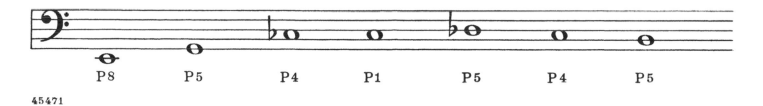

45471

The **MAJOR INTERVALS** are 2, 3, 6, 7. They are called Second, Third, Sixth, Seventh and are written M2, M3, M6, M7.

On the staff below, write Major Intervals over the notes given.

 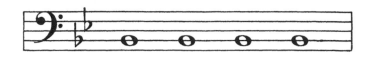

On the following staff are Major Intervals, Write their size under them.

Here are Major intervals in different keys. Remember to call the lower note *do* of the Major Key for each interval and write a note above it to make the size given.

M2   M3   M6   M7   M3   M6   M7

M3   M2   M6   M3   M3   M6   M7

Below are both Perfect and Major Intervals. Write P or M and the size below each interval.

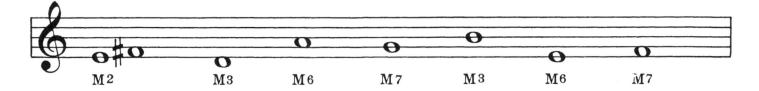

On the following staff, complete the intervals named.

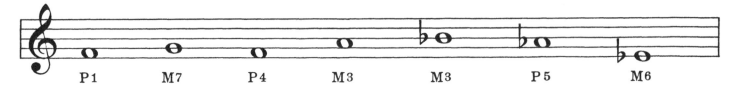

P1   M7   P4   M3   M3   P5   M6

Work Sheet

1   Name the two kinds of intervals in a Major Key.

_____   _____

2   Which kind are 2, 3, 6, 7?

3   What are the numbers of the other kind? _____

4   On the staff below, write the intervals for the scale of G in the Bass clef. Name and Number each interval.

5   Now write the intervals for the scale of F in the Treble clef. Name and Number each interval.

6   Write a note above each of the following notes to form their intervals.

P4   M3   P5   M7   P8   M6   M2

7   Which type of PITCH is more important, Absolute or Relative?

_____

8   Which scale degrees are the most important?

_____

Lesson Seven

FRANZ JOSEPH HAYDN

(1732-1809)

We have learned that Bach and Handel were the greatest of the early composers whose works for the Clavichord and Harpsichord are now played on the piano.

Haydn was one of the first composers to write for the piano. Because there were more keys on the piano and because it was possible to play either loud or soft, music writing changed. Some of Haydn's pieces are similar to the early dances, but his more difficult works helped other composers write great pieces for the piano.

Franz Haydn was born in a small town in Austria — the same year as George Washington. He came from a very poor family who loved music and played a little. When Franz was only five years old, his talent was easily seen. But there were no good music teachers in the town where he lived. An older cousin, who was a music teacher in a different town, took Franz to live with him and his wife. Here Franz learned to sing and to play the violin and other instruments.

The cousin's wife did not bother to look after Franz. The boy was often hungry, and his clothes were soiled and wrinkled. This made him sad as he had been well cared for by his own family. He did not understand why he could not live in his own home where he had been so happy.

When he was eight years old, he moved to Vienna to a school where he sang in the choir and learned more about music. Life was very hard for him here also, but he practiced on the harpsichord and composed music.

His voice broke when he was seventeen years old. This meant he could no longer stay at the school and sing in the choir. He then started to give music lessons to earn his living.

When he was twenty nine years old, he married a pupil of his. Franz had been in love with her sister but was too shy to tell her. The girl he loved entered a convent. The father of the girls persuaded Franz to marry the older girl. She was unkind to Franz and they lived apart.

Prince Esterhazy who always had good music at his court, hired Haydn. For twenty five years Haydn was busy playing, composing, and teaching. He became famous all over Europe. Then he moved to London where he became rich and even more famous. He was a friend of Mozart and Beethoven. Everyone loved him and called him "Papa Haydn."

We must be able to find the ROOT of a chord easily and to know its scale degree.

A triad in **ROOT POSITION** has its ROOT on the BOTTOM. If this note is on a line, the other notes are also on lines. If this note is on a space, the other notes are also on spaces.

A triad in **FIRST INVERSION** (a 6 chord) has its ROOT on the TOP.

A triad in **SECOND INVERSION** (a $\frac{6}{4}$ chord) has its ROOT in the MIDDLE.

When we know the Key Signature and the name of the ROOT, it is easy to tell the scale degree.

Remember the First Inversion has the interval of a 6th from the bottom note to the top note. The Second Inversion has an interval of a 4th from the bottom note to the next note above it and an interval of a 6th from the bottom to the top note.

On the following staff, mark the ROOT of each chord with R, and below the staff write the scale degree of the root. (Look at the key signature for *do*, then count to the root note.) Mark the inversions. The first has been done for an example. All the chords are I, IV or V.

On the staff below, do the same with the following triads. Notice that they are in the bass clef.

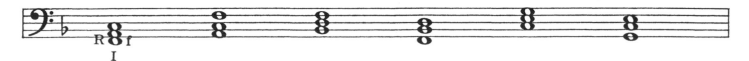

Play these triads on the piano.

Here is the melody of *My Darling Clementine* and some of its chords. Write in the chords where only the figure is given and write the Time Signature. Then play it on the piano.

Can you play this in other keys?

Write R for the roots of the following chords. Mark scale degrees and inversions under the chords.

Work Sheet

1   What are Haydn's other names? _____

2   Who was born the same year? _____

3   Write the chords and their inversions in the keys given.

    I   I6   I$^6_4$ IV   IV6   IV$^6_4$

4   Give the scale degrees and inversions of the following chords.

5   Write the chords for the figures given: Notice the keys.

    V   V6   V$^6_4$ IV   IV6   IV$^6_4$

6   Give the scale degrees and inversions of the following chords.

7   Write each INTERVAL's name and size in the Key of A.

Lesson Eight

WOLFGANG AMADEUS MOZART
(1756-1791)

Mozart (pronounced Mote Zart) was born in Salzburg, Austria. He began to play the clavier when he was three years old. His sister, Marianne, was five years older than he and was also very musical. Their father, Leopold Mozart was a musician and began to teach Marianne, or Nannerl as she was called, when she was seven years old.

Wolfgang would go to the clavier after his sister and play the same pieces. When he was four, his father gave him lessons also. He learned so fast that he became a wonderful player when he was only six years old.

Leopold took Nannerl and Wolfgang on concert tours. They played before kings and queens in France and England. Mozart started composing his beautiful music when he was only five years old. He learned to play the violin and the organ without any lessons.

He was a great genius. People would ask him to do very difficult things at the keyboard. But no matter how difficult, he was always able to play anything they wanted. He was equally good in his composing. He wrote every form of music: opera, orchestra, voice, violin, piano, organ. He wrote Church music, Symphonies, Operas, Concertos, Solos, Duets, Chamber Music, everything, and all of it is beautiful.

Although he was such a marvelous musician, he was unable to make a good living. Others were jealous of his ability. Also he was in poor health as was his fun-loving wife, Constance. He was always in debt. But, no matter how much trouble he had or how many worries over ill health and poverty, his music is always lovely. He believed music should delight people and make them happy.

Mozart was only 35 years old when he died. He was given a pauper's funeral. Fifty years later, a great institution was begun at Salzburg called the Mozarteum. Now there are branches of it many other places.

The Mozarteum has an orchestral society which plays Mozart's music in the churches of Salzburg. There are also twelve concerts a year and a music school where members of the orchestra teach students. Every summer great musicians teach at these Mozarteums. Every year during July and August Mozart is honored with festivals.

SEVENTH CHORDS AND INVERSIONS

A **SEVENTH CHORD** has FOUR letters of the Chord Alphabet.

    The top note is a 7th above the root.

    Below are two seventh chords in root position. Complete the others.

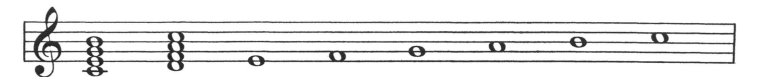

A SEVENTH CHORD has 4 tones. Therefore it has 4 positions.

    Root   1st inversion   2nd inversion   3rd inversion

It is very easy to find the root of a 7th chord. In root position, it is on the bottom. In all the inversions, the 7th note and the root are next to each other and form an interval of a second. The root is the higher of the two notes. See the examples above.

Markings for the inversions tell how far this second is from the lowest note. The two figures are the interval measurement from the lowest note to the 7th note and from the lowest note to the root. When the lowest note is the 7th, only one figure is given. See the examples above.

On the staff below, mark the inversions of the 7th chords.

It is very easy to find the root of a 7th chord. In root position, it is on the bottom. In all the inversions, the 7th note and the root are next to each other and form an interval of a second. The root is the higher of the two notes. See the examples above.

The seventh chord most often used is the **DOMINANT SEVENTH**. Its ROOT is the DOMINANT (V) of the key.

Key of C   V = G   Key of G   V = D

45471

38

On the staff below, write, then play, the Dominant 7th and its inversions in the Key of G. The chord is given in root position.

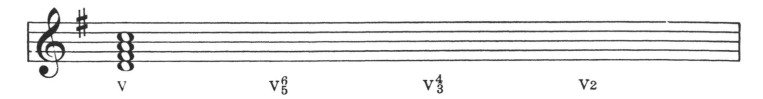

On the staff below, write, then play, the Dominant 7th and its inversions in the Key of F.

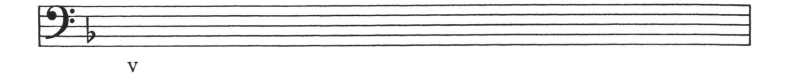

At the end of a composition, you will find the TONIC CHORD. Just before it you will usually find the DOMINANT or DOMINANT 7th CHORD. Sometimes only a few notes of the chords are used. Look at your music and check the last two chords.

Play the chords given below. Do they sound familiar?

The following shows how chords can be identified with no solid chords. This is the end of *Presto* by Wolfgang Amadeus Mozart. The second example is from the second of *Seven German Dances* by Joseph Haydn.

Work Sheet

1   What was the first name of Mozart's father? _____

2   Where was Mozart born? _____

3   How many years did he live? _____

4   How many tones are there in a 7th chord? _____

5   In the spaces, write the notes that form 7th chords.

_G_ ____ ____ ____ ,   _D_ ____ ____ ____

6   The DOMINANT 7th is a 7th on which scale degree?

7   Write the Dominant 7th, Root position, in the keys given:

8   Write the Dominant 7th, 1st inversion, in the keys given:

9   Write the Dominant 7th, 2nd inversion, in the keys given:

10 Write the Dominant 7th, 3rd inversion, in the keys given:

Lesson Nine

LUDWIG van BEETHOVEN

(1770-1827)

Ludwig van Beethoven was born in Bonn, Germany. Today people from all over the world go to Bonn to see the museum of Beethoven's possessions, including his piano.

Beethoven's father was a singer. His grandfather had been a court musician. His father heard that Leopold Mozart had made money by having his children play concerts when they were young. So he decided to do this with Ludwig. He drank a great deal and would often get poor Ludwig up in the middle of the night and make him practice until dawn.

When Ludwig was 8, he gave his first concert. His father advertised him as 6, thinking it would impress people more. Ludwig became an organist, assistant to the head organist, before he was 14 years old. He held this position until he was 22.

When he was 17, he visited Vienna for a few months where he met and played for Mozart. He returned to Bonn when his mother passed away. His father could not hold a job, and Beethoven had to support him.

When he was 22, Beethoven met Haydn in Bonn. Haydn helped Beethoven by telling a town offcial what a good musician he was. So Beethoven was sent to Vienna for music instruction.

Here he became famous and began giving concerts all over Europe. He played before kings and other important people and made many friends among the noblemen. A great deal of the music he composed was published.

When Beethoven was in his thirties, he started to lose his hearing. By the time he was fifty, he was completely deaf and could not hear his beloved music. For a while he stopped composing, but his love of music and his knowledge of harmony were so great that he began to compose again even though he could no longer hear!

Beethoven was a man of violent nature. Sometimes he would be very kind and friendly. Other times he would be quite mean. His music is like his moods—sometimes gentle, sometimes violent. His piano sonatas are especially famous. Some of his music can be played before you are very advanced in your playing, but a great deal of it is extremely difficult.

Below is *America* in the Key of G. Write in the chords where there is a figure but no chord. Write in the figures below chords without figures. Play this song on the piano.

42

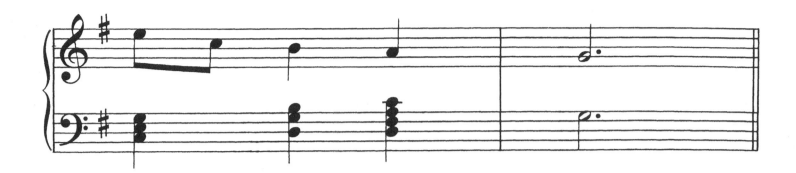

Write the chords above the following bass notes. Then play *Good Night, Ladies* on the piano.
Can you transpose this song to the key of G at the piano?

I_4^6 I_4^6 I_4^6 V7

I_4^6 IV6 I_4^6 V7 I_4^6

Many compositions are written on the I, IV, V or V7 chords,   including several Christmas
carols. If you can pick out the melody with your right hand and fit these chords where
they belong with your left hand, you will be able to play many songs "by ear."

As you learn pieces, see if you can recognize the chords in the piece and the chord pattern as well
as the themes.

45471

Work Sheet

1   Where was Beethoven born? _____

2   What was his first name? _____

3   What two very famous musicians did he know? _____

_____

4   What tragic thing happened to him? _____

_____

5   On the staff below, write chords on the figured bass. Play them.

6   On the staff below, write figures for the chords. Play them.

7   Write DOMINANT 7ths in the KEYS given below. Play them.

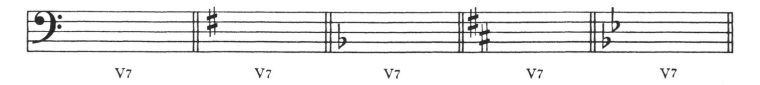

8   Write chords above the figures given. Play them.

45471

Lesson Ten

CADENCES

CADENCES are MUSICAL PUNCTUATION. Cadences are made of two or more chords.

Cadences separate ideas in music just as commas and periods separate ideas in words.

Cadences are important because they bring out the MEANING of the music.

Expression marks bring out the BEAUTY.

Accents bring out RHYTHM.

All of these are important for the best INTERPRETATION of music. Interpretation means to make others understand the music you are playing.

The last chord of a cadence is called the **CADENCE CHORD**.

The cadences easiest to find are at the end of a piece. This is usually V or V7 - I. This cadence is called an **AUTHENTIC CADENCE**. Play these on the piano.

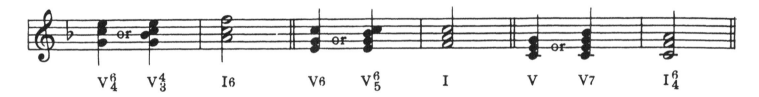

$$V_4^6 \qquad V_3^4 \qquad I6 \qquad V6 \qquad V_5^6 \qquad I \qquad V \qquad V7 \qquad I_4^6$$

On the staff below, write Authentic Cadences in the Key of G. Play them.

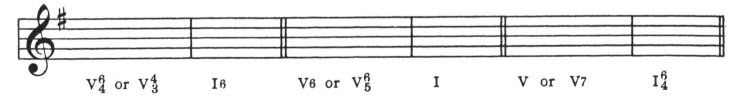

$$V_4^6 \text{ or } V_3^4 \qquad I6 \qquad V6 \text{ or } V_5^6 \qquad I \qquad V \text{ or } V7 \qquad I_4^6$$

Write and play these Authentic Cadences in the Key of C.

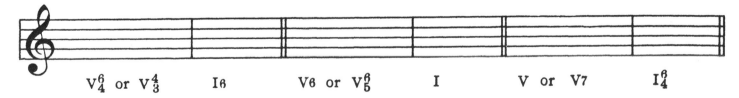

$$V_4^6 \text{ or } V_3^4 \qquad I6 \qquad V6 \text{ or } V_5^6 \qquad I \qquad V \text{ or } V7 \qquad I_4^6$$

Here are AUTHENTIC CADENCES in the Key of F. Play them on the piano. Notice that the single notes for the left hand are ROOTS of the chords. These are in addition to the three note chords for the right hand.

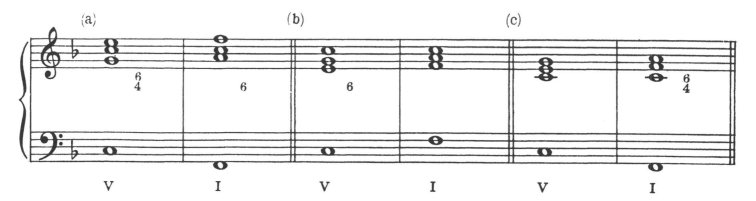

Below are the same authentic cadences but in the Key of C.

    Write in the two notes missing under each note in the treble clef.

    Play these cadences on the piano.

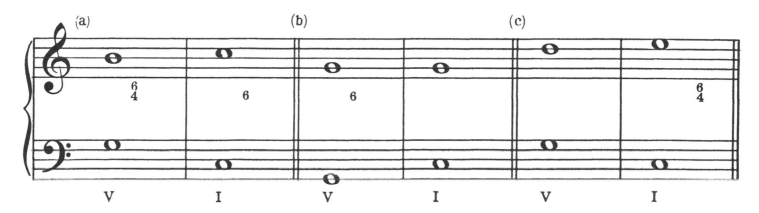

Below are the same authentic cadences in the Key of G.

    Write in the two notes missing under each note in the treble clef.

    Play these cadences on the piano.

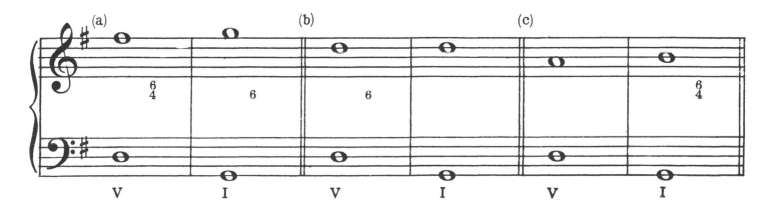

Look at the music you are learning. At the end there is probably an authentic cadence. . . either the full chords or parts of them. Notice that the CADENCE CHORD (last chord) has *do* at the top and at the bottom.

Now look at the cadences we have written on the preceding page. Notice that (a) of each set has *do* at the top and bottom. These are **PERFECT CADENCES**.

PERFECT CADENCES have *do* at the top and bottom. Or you can say– in the Soprano and the Bass.

Perfect cadences are like periods in sentences. They are the final punctuation. They are the STRONGEST cadences.

In the examples on the preceeding page, the cadences marked (b) and (c) the top or soprano does NOT have *do*. These are WEAK CADENCES and are called **IMPERFECT**. They are more like commas in sentences.

Below is *Merrily We Roll Along.* You can see that the chords in measures 3 and 4 are a WEAK CADENCE and the chords in measures 7 and 8 a STRONG CADENCE. Play this.

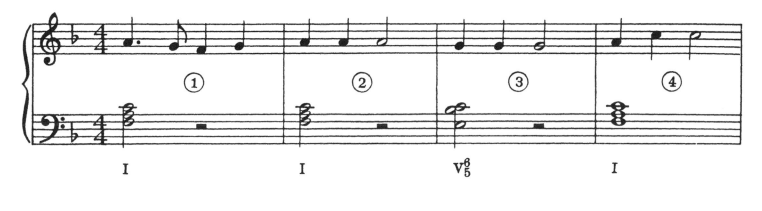

Can you transpose this piece to other keys?

Work Sheet

1   What are cadences? _____

2   How are they formed? _____

_____

3   Why are they important? _____

_____

4   Which chord is the CADENCE CHORD? _____

5   In an AUTHENTIC CADENCE which chord is before the Cadence Chord?

_____

6   In a PERFECT CADENCE in what two places do we find *do*?

_____

7   Check the STRONG CADENCE.   Perfect _____   Imperfect _____

8   In the following cadences, write P over the perfect ones and write I over the imperfect ones.

On the staffs below, write authentic cadences in the keys given.

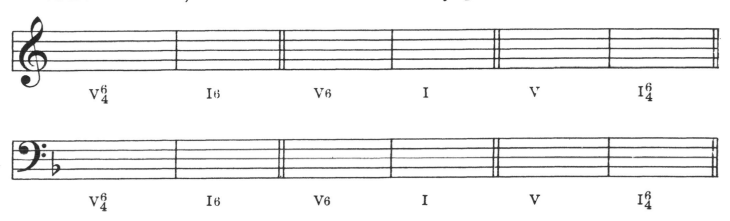

V_4^6 I_6 V_6 I V I_4^6

V_4^6 I_6 V_6 I V I_4^6

48

Examination

1   Write the Chromatic Scale one octave, going up.

2   What does DIATONIC mean? _____

3   What is a Scale Degree? _____

4   What is a STEP PATTERN of a Major Scale? _____

    _____

5   How many Tetrachords are there in a scale? _____

6   On the staff below, draw lines under the tetrachords which are the same and mark them *a* and *b*.

7   Write Key Tones *(do)* for the Signatures below.

8   Fill in the number of sharps or flats in the keys below.

    D ____   E ____   B ____   C♯ ____   B♭ ____   D♭ ____   E♭ ____   A ____

9   Write the ENHARMONIC NOTES for the following.

    C𝄪 ____   E ____   F♯ ____   A ____   B ____   D𝄪 ____   D♭♭ ____

10 Below is the Circle of _____ or _____ Circle. Write in the Key Tones.

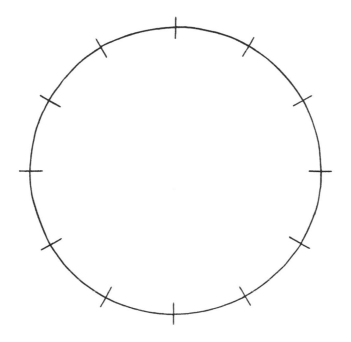

11 Give NAMES and NUMBERS of the 3 leading scale degrees.

12 Write these three notes for each of the keys given.

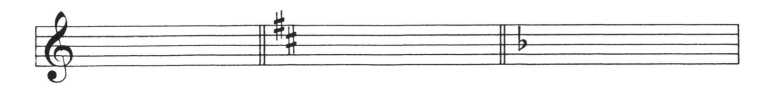

13 What are the TOP figures for SIMPLE TIME? _____ _____ _____

14 What is a TRIAD? _____

15 How many POSITIONS does it have? _____

16 Write the positions for the triads on C and G

17 What are these positions called? _____

_____

18 Write the numeral and inversion figures under the chords below.

I6

19 Write figures under the chords given. Write the chords over the figures below.

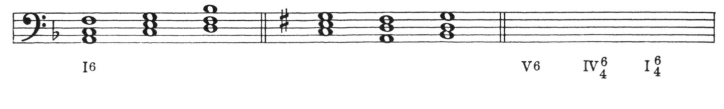

I6   V6   IV$^6_4$ I$^6_4$

20 How many tones are there in a 7th chord? _____

21 How many positions? _____

22 What scale degree is the ROOT of a Dominant 7th? _____

23 Write Dominant 7ths in Root Position for the keys given below.

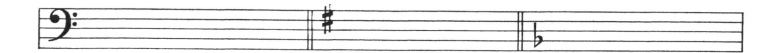

24 Mark the inversions of the 7th chords below.

25 Write the inversions of the 7th chord below. Root given.

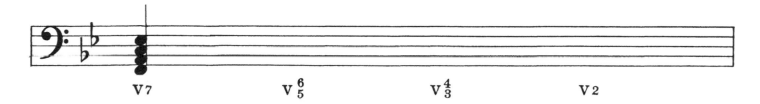

$$V_7 \qquad V\,{}^6_5 \qquad V\,{}^4_3 \qquad V\,2$$

26 Write R before the Root of the chords given below.

27 Check which is more important. Relative Pitch _____

     or Absolute Pitch _____

28 What is an INTERVAL? _____

_____

29 What are the intervals 1, 4, 5, 8? _____

30 What are the intervals 2, 3, 6, 7? _____

31 Write the names and size of the intervals below:

32 How are intervals used to show inversions of triads?

1st inv. _____   2nd inv. _____

33 How are they used to show inversions of 7th chords?

1st inv. _____   2nd inv. _____   3rd inv. _____

34 What two chords form an AUTHENTIC CADENCE?

_____ or _____   _____

35 What does a PERFECT CADENCE have in the soprano and bass? _____

36 Write which type is WEAK and which is STRONG.

PERFECT _____   IMPERFECT _____

37 In a composition, what do the following give?

Cadences _____

Expression Marks _____

Accents _____

38   Name the song below: _____

What is the Song Form? _____

Write in the Time Signature. Also write Chords for the figures and figures for the chords given. Then play it on the piano.

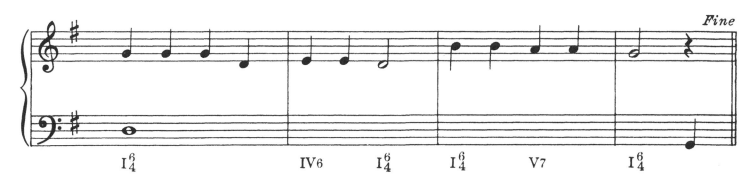